Prophetic Peace

Understanding End Times Without Fear

Bentley Thompson

Contents

INTRODUCTION: When the News Steals Your Peace

You're sitting on your couch, favorite beverage in hand, watching the evening news. Another war. Another economic crisis. Another pandemic scare. Your stomach tightens.

Searching for relief, you switch to YouTube. But here's another 'expert' you follow, explaining how this latest event is a sure sign of the end times. Your mind races.

Questions. *Is this it? Are we living in the last days? Am I ready? Is my family ready?*

A verse floats like fog in your head. You reach for your Bible—maybe Revelation, maybe Daniel—hoping for answers. But the symbols are confusing. The beasts and numbers and seals feel like a code you were never given the key to unlock. And now you're not just anxious about the news;

you're anxious about not understanding the very book that's supposed to bring you comfort.

If this sounds familiar, you're not alone.

Millions of Christians today are watching the same news headlines you are. They're seeing the same conflicting prophecy interpretations in supermarket checkout tabloids as well as in bookstores. They're feeling the same low-grade anxiety that whispers, "Something bad is coming, and I'm not prepared."

And here's what makes it worse: everyone seems to have a different answer. One preacher says the Antichrist is already here. Another says we're in the tribulation period. A third says Jesus is coming back next Tuesday at 3 p.m. (Okay, maybe not that specific, but you get the idea.) The noise is deafening. The confusion is paralyzing.

So, you're left wondering: Where is God in all this chaos? Has He lost control? Or worse—is He silent?

Here's the answer that might surprise you: What if the chaos we see in our world today isn't proof that God has lost control—it's proof that He's still very much in control?

What if the wars, the economic upheaval, the political turmoil, and yes, even the pandemics, aren't signs that we should panic—but indications that God's plan is unfolding exactly as He said it would?

What if biblical prophecy wasn't given to terrify you, but to give you peace?

That's what this book is about: **prophetic peace.**

Not the kind of peace that comes from ignoring the news or pretending everything is fine. It's not the peace that requires you to become a prophecy scholar or to memorize every apocalyptic timeline.

No—this is the peace that comes from understanding that the God who spoke the world into existence is the same God who holds your tomorrow in His hands. The peace that comes from realizing that every "scary" headline you read or hear is actually a confirmation that His Word is true.

We are talking about the peace that replaces anxiety with confident faith, one prophecy at a time.

I didn't always have this peace. I know what it feels like to be afraid of Bible prophecy and the apparent mixed bag of interpretations.

Some years ago, a coworker told me that when it came to Bible prophecy, he was a preterist. I didn't know what "preterist" meant at the time. I hadn't heard the word before.

We were on an assignment that required us to drive together from Atlanta, Georgia, to Chattanooga, Tennessee. For most of that two-hour ride, I just listened as he swung from prophecy to politics and back to prophecy—over and over again. I was worried that my ignorance on concepts like preterist, 'pre-tribulation', and 'post-tribulation' would leave me wearing a "Religiously Dumb" sticker on my back. (Hey, don't worry if you never heard those terms before either.)

Although I recognized some of the things he talked about, he rarely used the Bible to prove his points. He was flying on one wing, and I felt left out of a discussion that should have been grounded in Scripture.

Years later, I'm aware that several people may read the same passage in the Bible and come away with completely different understandings depending on what interpretive framework they subscribed to. One person sees the tribulation as past. Another sees it as future. A third sees it as symbolic. Same Bible passage. Different conclusions.

But here's the most important realization I came to—the Bible interprets itself. **We just need to read the whole thing in context.**

When I stopped relying on human interpretations and started letting Scripture explain Scripture, prophecy stopped being intimidating. It started being exactly what God intended it to be: *a source of hope, comfort, and peace.*

And that's what I want for you.

In this book, I'm going to show you how to find that same peace. We're going to walk through what I call the LIGHT framework—five principles drawn directly from 2 Peter 1:19.

But first, you need to know **why** Peter wrote these words—because the context changes everything.

Just before verse 19, Peter describes one of the most extra-ordinary experiences in human history. He, James, and John climbed a mountain with Jesus. And there, they witnessed something that would forever change how they understood prophecy.

Peter writes:

> "For we did not follow cunningly devised fables when we made known to you the power and com-ing of our Lord Jesus Christ, but were eyewitness-es of His majesty. [17] For He received from God the Father honor and glory when such a voice came to Him from the Excellent Glory: 'This is My beloved Son, in whom I am well pleased.' [18] And we heard this voice which came from heaven when we were with Him on the holy mountain."
>
> —2 Peter 1:16-18 (NKJV)

Do you know what Peter is describing? The **Transfigura-tion**—one of the most glorious moments recorded in Scrip-ture.

Jesus took Peter, James, and John up a mountain. There, His appearance was transformed before their eyes. Matthew tells us "*His face shone like the sun, and His clothes became as white as the light*" (Matthew 17:2). This wasn't a gentle glow. This was blazing, blinding, overwhelming glory—the radiance of God Himself shining through Jesus' humanity.

Then Moses and Elijah appeared beside Jesus—representing two classes of people who will be taken to heaven at the Second Coming of Christ: Moses was a token of those who will be resurrected. Elijah who had been taken to heaven alive (2 Kings 2:11) represented those who will not experience death and remain alive until Christ comes (see 1 Thessalonians 4:16-17). The Transfiguration event was encouragement to Jesus for His upcoming sacrifice. It also allowed the disciples to witness a miniature representation of the future kingdom of glory. The prophecies about the Messiah were being confirmed right before their eyes.

And then God the Father spoke audibly from heaven: "*This is My beloved Son, in whom I am well pleased. Hear Him!*" (Matthew 17:5)

Peter was so overwhelmed by what he was experiencing—the light, the glory, the divine presence—that he blurted out: "*Lord, it is good for us to be here; if You wish, let us make here three tabernacles: one for You, one for Moses, and one for Elijah*" (Matthew 17:4).

He didn't want to leave. He wanted to build shelters and stay in that glorious moment forever.

Can you imagine? Peter saw Jesus in His glorified state—the same glory He'll have when He returns. He heard God's voice.

He felt the weight of divine majesty pressing down on him. He experienced a preview of the Second Coming.

Now here's why I'm telling you this story in a book about finding peace in prophecy:

Because immediately after describing this mountain experience—immediately after testifying as an eyewitness to Jesus' glory—Peter writes:

> "And so we have the prophetic word confirmed, which you do well to heed as a light that shines in a dark place, until the day dawns and the morning star rises in your hearts."
>
> 2 Peter 1:19

Do you see the connection?

Peter is saying: "**I saw Jesus in His glorified state. I witnessed a preview of His second coming. I experienced the blinding light of His divine glory. And that experience CONFIRMS every prophetic promise about His return. The light I'm telling you to trust isn't just a metaphor—I SAW it with my own eyes.**"

The transfiguration wasn't just a special moment for three privileged disciples. It was God giving eyewitness testimony to the absolute certainty of Christ's return. Peter saw the Morning Star blazing in glory. He heard God's voice confirming Jesus' identity and mission. He felt overwhelmed by divine majesty.

And now he's writing to tell you: "**What I experienced on that mountain is coming back—for everyone. The dawn is real. The Morning Star will rise. I know this with absolute certainty, because I saw it.**"

This is why prophecy brings peace instead of panic.

It's not based on speculation or human wisdom. It's not built on "**cunningly devised fables**" (2 Peter 1:16). It's rooted in eyewitness testimony from someone who saw Jesus glorified—someone who witnessed a preview of the Second Coming—and is telling you with unshakable confidence: **He's coming back exactly as promised**.

When Peter tells you to pay attention to prophecy "*as a light that shines in a dark place*," he's not using poetic language. He's remembering the actual, physical, overwhelming LIGHT that radiated from Jesus on that mountain. He's remembering the glory that made him want to stay there forever.

And he's saying: "**That light is your guide through these dark times. That glory is what's coming. Trust it. I saw it. It's real.**"

This is the foundation of prophetic peace.

Not wishful thinking. Not blind optimism. Not ignoring reality.

But confident trust based on eyewitness testimony from someone who saw the future and came back to tell you: **"Don't be afraid. I've seen what's coming. It's glorious beyond words. Every prophecy points to that moment. You can trust the light."**

Here's the journey we'll take together:

L - **Left for Us** (WHO): You'll discover that biblical prophecy isn't just for scholars—it's God's gift to YOU, His beloved child.

I - **Instead of Panic** (WHAT): You'll learn what prophetic peace really is, and how it replaces fear with faith in God's sovereignty.

G - **Guiding Through Darkness** (WHY): You'll understand why prophecy brings peace instead of fear, and how to avoid the confusion paralyzing so many believers today.

H - **History Proves It** (WHERE): You'll see concrete proof that God has kept every prophetic promise so far—which means you can trust Him with the ones still ahead.

T - **Trusting Through the Headlines** (WHEN & HOW): You'll learn practical tools for watching current events unfold without panicking, and how to live with prophetic hope instead of prophetic dread.

You will push back the prophetic panic and dispel the confusing darkness by following the LIGHT "that shines in a dark place."

My prayer is that, by the time you finish this book you'll be able to turn on the news, look at the chaos, and go on with confidence—understanding that the news confirms everything God has outlined or predicted is right on schedule. God's still in control.

You won't need to avoid the book of Revelation anymore. You won't be intimidated by Daniel's visions. And you won't be tossed around by every new "prophetic interpretation" that goes viral on social media or broadcasted on popular TV channels.

Instead, you'll have something far more valuable: a **peace that surpasses understanding** (Philippians 4:7)—even when what's happening in the world around you doesn't make sense.

God hasn't left you in the dark. He's given you a light.

So, take a deep breath. Pour some more drink if you need to. And let's light up those headlines together.

Chapter One

L – Left For Us: Who Bible Prophecy Is Really For

You're wondering if prophecy is really for someone like you—a regular person trying to make sense of confusing symbols and scary predictions.

Let me answer that question clearly: Yes. Bible prophecy is for you.

In fact, the apostle Peter tells us that prophecy was left specifically for people like you and me:

> 'And so **we have the prophetic word confirmed**, which you do well to heed **as a light that shines in a dark place**, until the day dawns and the morning star rises in your hearts.'
>
> 2 Peter 1:19

Notice he doesn't say 'for scholars only' or 'for the spiritually advanced.' He says we—all of us—do well to pay attention to it. This is the **L** in our LIGHT framework: prophecy was **Left for Us**.

Prophecy Is God's Gift to His Children, not a Puzzle for Scholars

You hear of things happening all over the world—natural disasters, wars, mass killings. Fear and panic become your primary emotion. But you're a believer. So you think of the Bible, the prophecies. And things don't unravel.

You're thinking... The language in the newscasts is clearer than the words in the Bible. It feels like having the best luxury car in the garage, but you are not licensed, and you don't understand the controls. You can't drive. You're stuck.

But what if you're not unlicensed at all? What if the key has been in your hand the whole time—you just didn't know it?"

Rest assured, this is for YOU—not just seminary professors or prophecy experts.

Scripture tells us, '*Surely the Lord God does nothing, unless He reveals His secret to His servants the prophets*' (Amos 3:7). Think about that: God doesn't act in secret. He tells His people what He's planning—not because He has to, but because He loves us and wants us included in what He's doing. The gift of Prophecy has been **left for us as a light to illuminate and to guide**.

If prophecy were only for the "elite," God wouldn't have put it in a book for everyone to read.

God Doesn't Leave His Children in the Dark About the Future

Picture a loving father preparing his kids for a long road trip. He knows they'll get anxious as the miles stretch on. He knows they'll ask the inevitable question: 'Are we there yet?'

So what does he do? He gives them a map. He tells them what to expect. 'We'll see mountains here, cross a river there, stop for lunch around noon.' Not because he wants to spoil the surprise, but because knowing the plan helps them enjoy the journey.

God gave prophecy so we wouldn't "languish in despair, without hope". Bible prophecy has been left for us—for every believer.

The opposite of prophetic knowledge isn't blissful ignorance—it's paralyzing anxiety. And God knows this. Peter understood this on the deepest level. After witnessing Jesus' transfiguration—after seeing Him glorified on the mountain with his own eyes, after hearing God's voice declare "This is My beloved Son"—Peter could have kept that experience private. It was personal, sacred, overwhelming.

But instead, decades later, he wrote about it (2 Peter 1:16-18). Why? Because he wanted **you** to have the same confidence that experience gave him. He wanted you to know that prophecy isn't speculation or religious theory. The prophets' prediction of Christ's return was confirmed by eyewitness testimony from someone who saw a pre-view of the Second Coming.

Peter saw the Morning Star blazing in glory. He witnessed Jesus transfigured in light brighter than the sun. And he's writing to tell you: "This is real. This is coming. You can trust every prophetic promise because I saw where it's all leading."

That's a Father's heart.

God gave Peter that **mountaintop experience** not just for Peter's benefit, but so Peter could strengthen **your** faith. Prophecy was left for you—confirmed by those who witnessed Jesus' glory firsthand and came down from the mountain to tell you: "Don't be afraid. We've seen what's coming. It's glorious."

This is why Paul could write with such confidence:

> "Do not be anxious about anything, but in everything by prayer and pleading with thanks-giving let your requests be made known to God. And the peace of God, which surpasses all com-prehension, will guard your hearts and minds in Christ Jesus."
>
> Philippians 4:6-7 (NASB)

Notice the clear counsel—'Do not be anxious about any-thing...' That includes the future. That includes the news. That includes prophecy.

And here's the promise: when we bring our anxieties to God—including our fears about the end times—His peace will guard our hearts and minds. This peace is so profound it 'surpasses all comprehension.' You'll watch the news and not be overwhelmed. People may wonder how you can be so calm!

In His Sermon on the Mount, Jesus spoke directly to this anxiety:

> 'Do not worry about your life... Look at the birds of
> the air; for they neither sow nor reap nor gather
> into barns; yet your heavenly Father feeds them.
> Are you not of more value than they?'
> Matthew 6:25-26 (NKJV)

If God cares for birds and clothes the flowers how much more does He care about you—His beloved child who wants to understand His plans?

So let me ask you something: **Is God your Father?**

If your answer is yes—and I believe it is—then ask yourself this: **Is He a good Father?** The kind who prepares His children for what's ahead? The kind of Father who gives them what they need to face the future with confidence?

Of course He is. And a Father like that doesn't leave His children in the dark.

Some people think we must know every detail of every prophecy in order to be confident about the future. But that would make God a vending machine—insert prayer, get answers. That's not relationship; that's transaction.

No. God doesn't give us everything we want. Some knowledge is too great for us, and some questions are better left in His hands. But He gives us exactly what we need: enough light to take the next step, enough truth to build our faith, and enough promises to replace our fear with peace.

Therefore, we should expect that we will understand—not just what we want to understand—but what He chooses to reveal.

Prophecy Is Your Birthright as a Believer

Many years ago, when I was a physics instructor, I mentioned to my class that Isaac Newton—yes, that Newton—spent as much time studying biblical prophecy as he did to study mathematics and physics.

After class, several students wanted to talk more about prophecy. One student was particularly intrigued about John and the book of Revelation. She consulted her religious advisor—a priest, about Revelation and its strange symbols of beasts, seals, etc. The priest told her she should not be concerned about the book of Revelation because John was a senile old man when he wrote Revelation.

That was unfortunate because there are at least two clear clues every reader may pick up in the first few verses. First, the book is "**The Revelation of Jesus Christ...**" — Revelation 1:1. And the second?

You should read it. I would not risk presenting a damaged paraphrase. It says;

> "Blessed is he who reads and those who hear the words of this prophecy and keep those things which are written in it; for the time is near."
>
> Revelation 1:3 (NKJV)

There's a blessing promised to those who read, hear, and keep what John wrote in *'The Revelation of Jesus Christ'*.

Think about that word: *revelation*. It means unveiling, not concealing. Disclosing, not hiding.

So, when people say, 'Revelation is too mysterious to understand,' they've missed the whole point. It's called Revelation because God is revealing something, not hiding it.

Is that why 2 Peter 1:19 — the verse that inspired the *LIGHT Framework*—says we "do well" to pay attention? Studying the prophecies of the Bible is wise, not weird.

Bible prophecy is your birthright as a believer. Jesus wants you to know. He knows those who would be living in the end times would be anxious about the happenings. That's why He gave us Revelation—it's the Revelation of Jesus Christ. Christ and His plans for you are revealed in the prophecies of Revelation.

Even though some may say you won't be able to understand it—that you are not qualified or that you are just continuing to wade through the swamp of ideas and private interpretations—the very first verses in the book of Revelation show that those prophecies were **left for us**.

Rest assured, when you read the prophecies using the LIGHT framework in this book, you're not intruding on forbidden knowledge; you're accepting an invitation to know your Father's heart.

Chapter Two

I - Instead of Panic: What Is Prophetic Peace?

What is prophetic peace? And how is it different from the anxiety you feel when you watch the news?

Let me start with a story.

Some time back, I was late for work because there was a terrible accident at a busy intersection. Usually, if the accident scene involves any fatality, the whole thoroughfare is blocked until the scene is cleared.

I had to take a detour. Later that morning when I arrived at work, I learned that it was a collision involving two vehicles—one was T-boned and rolled over causing the death of the driver.

I thought, 'How unfortunate for those families!' I couldn't help thinking that if that victim had known it would be their last morning, their last drive down that familiar road, they would have chosen to stay home.

And that's the heart of our human dilemma, isn't it? We desperately want to know the future—especially when the present feels dangerous and uncertain. We think if we could just see what's coming, we could protect ourselves, prepare ourselves, control our destiny.

But here's the problem: our foreknowledge, at best, is still conjecture. Pure guesswork. We can't see into the future with certainty. We don't know what will happen even one second from now.

God does. And that changes everything.

God Understands Why Uncertainty Causes Anxiety

Here's something fascinating: research shows that uncertainty doesn't just make us uncomfortable—it intensifies our negative emotions. Studies from Spain and Germany found that nine out of ten people would rather not know about negative events in their future. Even more surprising? Forty to seventy percent preferred to remain ignorant about positive future events too.

Why? Because uncertainty itself—the not knowing—creates more anxiety than almost anything else.

Regardless of the possible outcomes, we never like uncertainty. We want to have as much hope as possible—whether in playing sports or undergoing a medical procedure.

Other research confirms this. When our brains can't predict what's coming, they perceive the future as 'separate' from us, making it nearly impossible to prepare or plan. This triggers a cascade of fear and worry.

As we watch the news and see wars, economic crises, natural disasters, such as hurricane devastation, flooding, wild fires, and social unrest, we don't know what's coming next or how bad it will get. That uncertainty—that darkness about the future—is paralyzing sometimes.

But here's what I want you to understand: God knew we would struggle with this. He designed us with the ability to think about the future, which means He also knew we'd worry about it.

And that's exactly why He gave us prophecy—not to tease us with mystery, but to graciously unpack enough of the unknown to calm our fears.

So how do we move from paralyzing uncertainty to prophetic peace?

Prophetic Peace Comes from Trusting God's Proven Word

Here's the key: uncertainty is inevitable, but trust in God's provision transforms fear into peace.

And this is what makes biblical prophecy different from every other attempt to predict the future: Bible prophecy isn't like weather predictions. It's what God already sees and has decided to allow to happen. Like a loving Father, He may choose to bring certain things to our consciousness so that we may know He is with us and is working for us.

Bible prophecy is not just foretelling of future events. It is a means of building our trust and faith in a God who is:
— omniscient (knows everything—present, past, and future),
— omnipotent (has all power), and
— omnipresent (is everywhere, at once!)

To have such faith in a Being Who does not physically live next door to us, requires a lot of evidence.

Prophecy provides such evidence. We build trust "one prophecy at a time" by seeing what God already fulfilled. But how do we know if a prophet is truly from God? Scripture gives us several tests, but here's one non-negotiable requirement:

> "When a prophet speaks in the name of the LORD, if the thing does not happen or come to pass, that is the thing which the LORD has not spoken; the prophet has spoken it presumptuously; you shall not be afraid of him."
>
> – Deuteronomy 18:22 (NKJV)

In other words: the predictions or prophecies of true prophets are never wrong. If someone claims to speak for God and their prediction doesn't come to pass, God didn't send them. Period.

Now, this test alone doesn't prove someone IS a true prophet—there are other requirements like consistency with Scripture and godly character. But it does prove when someone is NOT. A true prophet must have 100% accuracy—better than any meteorologist giving your daily weather forecast.

Bible prophecy, therefore, is God speaking to people through the medium called a prophet. Then He said, "**Hear now My words: If there is a prophet among you, I, the LORD, make Myself known to him in a vision; I speak to him in a dream.**" — Numbers 12:6 (NKJV)

So when the prophet Daniel interpreted the dream by the Babylonian king and outlined the succession of world kingdoms to follow Babylon, he wasn't stating a probability or making an educated guess. He was declaring absolute certainty:

'The dream is certain, and its interpretation is sure.' (Daniel 2:45, last part)

Read that again: **certain** and **sure**. Not maybe. Not probably. Not 'if current trends continue.' Daniel was saying, 'This is what God sees, and this is what will happen—guaranteed.'

And history proved him right. Every single kingdom Daniel named rose and fell exactly as predicted; over the course of 2,600 years.

So here's what this means for you today: When you read biblical prophecy, you're not reading someone's best guess about the future. You're reading what God—who sees the end from the beginning—has chosen to reveal. That's why it brings peace instead of anxiety.

Here's another example of God declaring something that would happen later in the future. Amazing!

> "But you, Bethlehem Ephrathah, Though you are little among the thousands of Judah, Yet out of you shall come forth to Me The One to be Ruler in Israel, Whose goings forth are from of old, From everlasting."
>
> – Micah 5:2 (NKJV)

The prophet Micah, writing approximately 700 years before Christ, declared that the Messiah would be born in Bethlehem; a tiny village, not the expected Jerusalem.

Here's what makes this remarkable: Just days before Jesus' birth, Mary and Joseph were 90 miles away in Nazareth with no reason to travel. Mary was in late pregnancy—dangerous travel conditions. They had no ties to Bethlehem except ancient ancestry.

Then a Roman emperor, ruling a foreign empire, with no knowledge of Jewish prophecy, issued a census decree that forced this couple to travel to the exact village Micah had named 700 years earlier. And they arrived just in time for Jesus to be born there.

The probability of all those factors aligning by coincidence? Humanly speaking, practically zero. But God said it through Micah, and it happened—exactly as He said.

Isaiah 46:9-10 shows God's unique credential: He declares the end from the beginning.

> Remember the former things of old, For I am God, and there is no other; I am God, and there is none like Me, [10]**Declaring the end from the beginning**, And from ancient times things that are not yet done, Saying, 'My counsel shall stand, And I will do all My pleasure,'
>
> Isaiah 46:9-10 (NKJV)

"God is never wrong. And He's never mistaken. He's never taken by surprise, and you'll never hear Him say, "Oops! I messed up." He always knows what is and what will be.

This means that the prophets who speak for God must also be correct in their prophecies 100% of the time! If not, they are not connected to the source of truth.

Peter's Unshakable Confidence (And Why It Should Give You the Same)

Let me tell you why Peter had such confidence in prophecy—confidence he desperately wanted to pass on to you.

Before writing 2 Peter 1:19, Peter made this bold declaration:

"For we did not follow cunningly devised fables when we made known to you the power and coming of our Lord Jesus Christ, but were eyewitnesses of His majesty." (2 Peter 1:16)

Peter wasn't theorizing about Jesus' return. He wasn't speculating based on ancient texts. He wasn't following popular teachings or sensational predictions from self-proclaimed prophets.

He was testifying as an eyewitness.

What did he witness? The event we now call the Transfiguration—recorded in Matthew 17:1-8, Mark 9:2-8, and Luke 9:28-36.

Here's what happened:

Six days after Peter confessed that Jesus was "the Christ, the Son of the living God" (Matthew 16:16), Jesus took Peter, James, and John up a high mountain. There, the extraordinary event occurred.

Matthew describes it: *"He was transfigured before them. His face shone like the sun, and His clothes became as white as the light"* (Matthew 17:2).

Mark adds: *"His clothes became shining, exceedingly white, like snow, such as no launderer on earth can whiten them"* (Mark 9:3).

Luke tells us: *"The appearance of His face was altered, and His robe became white and glistening"* (Luke 9:29).

This wasn't a gentle, peaceful glow like candlelight. This was blazing, blinding, transformative glory—the glory of God Himself radiating from Jesus' humanity. The same glory that filled the temple in the Old Testament. The same glory that will fill the earth when Jesus returns.

Peter was seeing a preview of the Second Coming.

But that wasn't all.

Suddenly, two figures appeared beside Jesus: Moses and Elijah. These two representatives are types of those who will be with Jesus at the Second Coming. Moses represented those who will be resurrected from death at the 'sound of the trumpet.' Those who would never have died (like Elijah)

— who would have remained alive until Jesus comes are the second group (see 1 Thessalonians 4:16-18).

And what were they discussing with Jesus? Luke tells us they "spoke of His decease which He was about to accomplish at Jerusalem" (Luke 9:31). They were talking about His upcoming death and resurrection—the fulfillment of every Messianic prophecy.

Every Old Testament promise was being confirmed before Peter's eyes.

Then, as if this weren't overwhelming enough, a bright cloud overshadowed them. And from the cloud came the voice of God the Father:

> *"This is My beloved Son, in whom I am well pleased. Hear Him!"*
>
> Matthew 17:5

Peter heard the voice of God. Not in his head. Not in his heart. Audibly. Out loud. Confirming everything Jesus had taught.

The disciples were so terrified they fell on their faces. When they looked up, Moses and Elijah were gone. Jesus was alone with them, looking normal again. And they descended the mountain in stunned silence.

Now, here's the part most people miss:

Peter was so overwhelmed by what he experienced that before God spoke from the cloud, he blurted out: *"Lord, it is good for us to be here; if You wish, let us make here three tabernacles: one for You, one for Moses, and one for Elijah"* (Matthew 17:4).

He wanted to stay there forever.

He wanted to build shelters, set up camp, and never leave that glorious moment. Why go back down to the world of sin and suffering and confusion when he could stay in the presence of divine glory?

But Jesus brought him back down the mountain. Because Peter's calling wasn't to stay in the experience—it was to share the hope of that experience with others.

And that's exactly what Peter did decades later when he wrote 2 Peter.

Do you see now why he could write with such confidence?

> *"And so we have the prophetic word **confirmed**, which you do well to heed as a light that shines in a dark place, until the day dawns and the morning star rises in your hearts."*
>
> 2 Peter 1:19

"Confirmed" by what? By what he witnessed on that mountain.

Peter saw Jesus glorified. He saw a preview of the glory Christ will have when He returns "*in His glory, and all the holy angels with Him*" (Matthew 25:31). He experienced the reality that every prophecy points toward.

And after seeing that glory, after hearing God's voice, after feeling the weight of divine majesty, Peter is writing to tell **you**:

"I know prophecy is true because I saw it. I witnessed Jesus in His coming glory. The Morning Star is real—I saw Him shining like the sun. The dawn is coming—I heard God confirm it. You can trust these prophetic promises because I was there, and what I saw confirms everything."

This is why Peter uses light imagery throughout 2 Peter 1:19.

He's not being poetic or metaphorical. He's remembering the actual, physical, overwhelming LIGHT that radiated from Jesus on that mountain. When he says prophecy is "*a light that shines in a dark place,*" he's thinking of the blinding glory that made him shield his eyes.

When he says "*until the day dawns and the morning star rises,*" he's remembering Jesus' face shining like the sun at dawn—so bright he could barely look at it.

These aren't just pretty words. They're eyewitness descriptions.

And Peter is saying to every anxious believer watching terrifying news headlines: **"That light is coming back. The darkness of this world is temporary. The Morning Star will rise**—not just on a mountain for three disciples, but everywhere, for everyone who trusts in Him."

This is the confidence Peter wants you to have.

Not second-hand confidence based on someone else's interpretation of current events. Not anxiety-filled speculation about whether we're in the end times. Not fear-driven obsession with prophetic timelines.

But rock-solid, eyewitness-testimony confidence that says: **"I know where prophecy is leading because someone I trust saw the destination."**

Think about this for a moment:

Peter wasn't afraid of Jesus' return. He **longed** for it. Why? Because he'd already seen the glory waiting at the end of the prophetic timeline. He'd experienced the overwhelming beauty, majesty, and peace of Jesus' glorified presence.

When you've seen that, you don't dread the Second Coming. You anticipate it. You watch for it. You hope for it with every fiber of your being.

That's what Peter experienced. And that's what he's offering you through his testimony.

When you read 2 Peter 1:19, you're not just reading doctrine or theology or nice religious sentiments.

You're reading the testimony of a man who:
— Saw Jesus glorified in blinding light
— Heard God's voice from heaven
— Witnessed Moses and Elijah (aligning with the promise in 1 Thessalonians 4:16-17)
— Experienced a preview of the Second Coming
— Wanted to stay in that moment forever

And Peter is now writing to tell you: **"Don't be afraid of prophecy. Don't let confusing interpretations or scary headlines steal your peace. I've seen what's coming. It's glorious beyond words. Every prophecy points to that moment. Trust the light. I saw it. It's real. And it's worth waiting for."**

This is prophetic peace.

Not a naive optimism that ignores reality. Not blind faith that refuses to ask questions.

But confident trust based on eyewitness testimony from someone who saw Jesus in His glory and came back to tell you: **"The Morning Star is rising. The dawn is breaking. What I witnessed on that mountain is what you're living toward. Don't be troubled. I've seen the end of the story. God wins. Light conquers darkness. And you get to be there when it happens."**

That's the confidence we're building in this book—one prophecy at a time.

A Quick Note About Conditional Prophecies

Now, you might be thinking: 'Wait, didn't Jonah prophesy that Nineveh would be destroyed in three days—and it wasn't? Doesn't that make him a false prophet by the Deuteronomy 18:22 test?'

Good question. Here's the key: Jonah brought a conditional prophetic message. The implied condition was 'Repent, or Nineveh will be destroyed.' When the city repented, God showed mercy.

Listen to God's heart through the prophet Ezekiel:

> Say unto them, As I live, saith the Lord God, I have no pleasure in the death of the wicked; but that the wicked turn from his way and live: turn ye, turn ye from your evil ways; for why will ye die, O house of Israel?
>
> – Ezekiel 33:11 (KJV)

God takes no pleasure in punitive executive judgment. His warnings are invitations to turn back to Him. When people respond in repentance, He responds in mercy.

So Jonah was an unwilling prophet, but not a false prophet. The prophecy was true, and Nineveh's repentance proved God's character.

Prophetic Peace Replaces Fear with Faith

Every day the news headlines scream chaos, while Bible prophecy whispers peace. It's easy to forget that God's still in control.

Increasingly, many Christians are expressing mixed feelings as they look at the wars, political polarization, environmental disasters, and global instability through the lens of faith and biblical prophecy.

Too often these situations are colored to make us panic—what is not explained away with scientific postulations is blamed on political opponents or enemy nations.

That is why you need to filter world events through the Bible's own explanation of its prophetic messages. To go by any individual's private interpretation—regardless of how popular or well-regarded they might be—is to increase the noise and intensify the panic.

Think about what Jesus said in Matthew 24:6:

> "And you will hear of wars and rumors of wars. See that you are not troubled; for all these things must come to pass, but the end is not yet."

Read that carefully. Jesus didn't say, 'IF you hear of wars.' He said, 'You WILL hear of wars and rumors of wars.'

He was predicting exactly what we see on the news every night. Wars. Conflicts. Rumors of more wars. And then He gave a direct command: '**See that you are not troubled.**'

Why? Because this is part of the plan to allow us to see the heinousness of sin; from which He wants to save us. These things '*must come to pass*.' The chaos isn't evidence that God lost control—it's evidence that He's still following the script He wrote.

And here's a truth to cling to when the news makes it seem like all of humanity is out of control:

'*The Most High rules in the kingdom of men*.' —Daniel 4:17, said Daniel (called Belteshazzar) to King Nebuchadnezzar.

Not 'ruled' past tense. Not 'will rule' future tense. Rules—present tense, active, right now. Never a time when God isn't Ruler.

Even when it doesn't look like it. Even when dictators rage and democracies crumble. Even when wars erupt and economies collapse, the Most High rules.

Prophetic Peace Prepares Believers for God's Work

Have you ever wondered how the prophet Daniel and his companions stayed so calm in the face of a den of lions and a super-heated furnace? Were they superhuman? Were they just naturally brave?

No. They had prophetic peace. They knew God's character. They knew His promises. They'd studied His Word and seen His faithfulness in the past.

That's why they could face death without panic. Not because they were tougher than you—but because they were more confident in God than in their circumstances.

Note that studying and believing the word of God causes our faith to grow. That's according to Romans 10:17.

And so, listen to this pillow-soft comfort from the word of God—

> **Be anxious for nothing**, but in everything by prayer and supplication, with thanksgiving, let your requests be made known to God; [7]and **the peace of God**, which **surpasses all understanding**, will guard your hearts and minds through Christ Jesus.
>
> Philippians 4:6-7 (NKJV)

In other words, *don't be anxious*. Instead of dreading the unknown, we can find reasons in Bible prophecy to help us live "ready and alert" (1 Thessalonians 5:4-6).

The passage says, with the word of God, "*you are not in darkness.*" We are all "*children of light,*" and all we need to do is "*watch and be sober.*"

That watchfulness is what makes us ready for service. It's the reason God's prophets—the ones we read of in the Bible—were so active. They shared messages of comfort. They delivered words of warning and rebuke. And, of course, they predicted future events.

Now we have the sure word of prophecy. And how is this prophetic word related to Christ? Revelation 19:10 says "the *testimony of Jesus is the spirit of prophecy*"—true prophecy points us to Christ. It's not surprising that the Book of Revelation begins, "The Revelation of Jesus Christ..." (Revelation 1:1).

It's all about Christ. Prophecy is not about fear and panic—it's about Him.

And when you understand that, it produces the peace Paul described in Philippians 4:6-7—a peace that surpasses all understanding, even when the world is falling apart around you.

That's prophetic peace. And it's yours for the taking.

Instead of panic, you can have peace. Instead of fear, you can have faith. Instead of anxiety about the future, you can have confidence in the One who holds the future.

Prophecy isn't just a survival guide for dark times. It's a hope-filled declaration that the darkness won't last. The Morning Star is coming (2 Peter 1:19, Revelation 22:16), and with Him comes the eternal kingdom where God's people will live in His light forever.

G - Guiding Through Darkness: Why Prophecy Brings Peace and Not Fear

Why does prophecy bring peace instead of fear? And why do so many people get it wrong?

Let me tell you a story that helps us answer both questions.

It was the night before Halloween, 1938. There was no social media yet. No network television, either. Families gathered around their radios, expecting music or the Sunday drama hour. Instead, a calm news voice broke in: "Ladies and gentlemen, we interrupt this broadcast to bring you an important bulletin..."

Reports followed about strange explosions on Mars—then of mysterious cylinders falling on a New Jersey farm. Soon came terrified "eyewitness" accounts of monstrous creatures attacking the countryside.

Listeners didn't know they were hearing a play. It was Orson Welles's dramatic adaptation of The War of the Worlds.

Those who tuned in late missed the opening disclaimer that it was a fictional presentation. Within minutes, fear spread like wildfire. People fled their homes, clogged the highways, and prayed in churches. Newspapers later exaggerated the chaos, but the lesson stood clear: panic thrives where understanding is absent.

One misunderstood broadcast had turned ordinary people into refugees from an invasion that never happened! The lesson? Confusion, not calamity, often ignites the strongest fear.

And that's exactly what's happening with biblical prophecy today. You don't panic because prophecy itself is scary. You do because you're confused about what it means. Clarity brings peace. Confusion brings fear.

So in this chapter, we're going to clear up the confusion.

The Fear Comes from Misunderstanding Symbolic Language

Think about your own experience with prophetic books like Daniel and Revelation. Beasts with multiple heads. Numbers like 666 and 1,260. Seals, trumpets, bowls. It feels like a secret code only experts can crack, doesn't it?

This intimidation keeps ordinary believers—people like you—from the very comfort God intended prophecy to bring.

Misunderstanding isn't new. Even in Bible times, spiritual leaders sometimes completely misread what was right in front of them.

Let me show you what I mean. In 1 Samuel 1, there's a woman named Hannah who desperately wanted a child. There was a situation where the high priest completely misunderstood her. His name was Eli and he had seen Hannah in the temple seemingly talking to herself.

After her husband showed his misunderstanding of her anguish, then came Eli who misinterpreted her silent prayer for drunkenness. Just as how the priest misinterpreted Hannah's silent prayer for drunken behavior, many Bible students misunderstand the symbols used in prophecies.

Think about this: Eli was the high priest—the most spiritually qualified person in Israel. He had decades of experience. He knew the Scriptures. He served in God's temple.

And yet he completely misread what was happening right in front of him. He saw a desperate woman pouring out her heart to God and called her a drunk.

Why? Because he didn't look carefully. He made assumptions. He jumped to conclusions.

The same thing happens with prophecy today. Well-meaning Bible teachers—sincere, experienced, even highly educated—can completely misread what God is saying. They see beasts and numbers and seals, make assumptions based on current events or popular theories, and miss what the prophet actually meant.

But it doesn't have to be that way. Just as Hannah's sincere prayer had meaning that Eli could have understood if he'd looked more carefully, biblical prophecy has clear meaning we can understand if we use the right approach.

A high priest misreads a sincere prayer as drunkenness. Today, many people read the prophetic books of the Bible and see other than what the prophet meant. But that does not have to be.

Today, the uncertainty associated with prophetic pronouncements, and the misinterpretations, like a hit-and-miss sport, can deprive us of the very comfort God intended for us.

Here's an important truth: God doesn't speak in riddles to confuse us—He uses symbols to reveal truth across time and cultures.

Think about it: A beast representing a kingdom makes sense whether you lived in Daniel's day or live in ours. A woman representing a church or city translates across centuries. Symbols are universal; specific names and details change.

But here's what Paul reminds us in 1 Corinthians 2:14:

> 'But the natural man does not receive the things of the Spirit of God, for they are foolishness to him; nor can he know them, because they are spiritually discerned.'

This doesn't mean you need a theology degree to understand Bible prophecy. It means you need a humble heart and a willingness to let Scripture interpret itself. Spiritual things are spiritually discerned—through prayer, study, and submission to God's will, not through human cleverness or popular theories.

Prophecy Addresses Our God-Given Need to Know the Future

God designed us with the capacity to think about past and future—this is part of being made in His image. We're not like animals that live only in the present moment. We plan. We anticipate. We prepare.

But with that gift comes a burden: We also worry about what we cannot see or control. We fear the unknown future.

Remember the research from Chapter 2? Uncertainty intensifies anxiety. Not knowing what's coming paralyzes us. This isn't a character flaw, per se—it's how we're wired. We NEED to know enough about the future to function with confidence in the present.

In a perfect world, we would be perfectly at ease with our confinement to the present. But this world is not perfect—neither are we.

And God knows this about us. That's exactly why He gave prophecy.

Prophecy isn't God teasing us with mystery—it's God graciously unpacking the unknown to calm our fears. He reveals what we need to know: that He's in control, that He has a plan, that the chaos we see is temporary, and that His kingdom will triumph in the end.

He doesn't tell us everything (we couldn't handle it), but He tells us enough. Enough to trust Him. Enough to find peace. Enough to watch the news without panicking.

Scripture Warns Against "Private Interpretation" for Good Reason

Let's return to our foundational verse in 2 Peter 1:19:

> 'We have the prophetic word confirmed, which you do well to heed as a light that shines in a dark place.'

You will agree—sometimes the desire to know what lies ahead is quite strong. It's in these times that Bible students must be careful.

God offers prophecy as a LIGHT—not as darkness, not as confusion, but as illumination. That's His intent.

But then verse 20 gives us a critical warning:

> 'Knowing this first, that no prophecy of Scripture
> is of any private interpretation.'

What does '*private interpretation*' mean? It means we can't just read a prophetic passage and decide for ourselves what it means based on our own ideas, current events, or creative theories.

Prophecy isn't a Rorschach test where everyone sees something different. It's not a puzzle where every Bible student comes up with their own solution. God has one meaning in mind—and He reveals it through the rest of Scripture.

That's why we have hundreds of conflicting interpretations today. Everyone has their 'private take' on the mark of the beast, the identity of the Antichrist, the timing of the rapture, the meaning of the millennium.

And all that confusion—all that conflicting noise—is exactly what makes some people anxious. They don't know who to believe anymore.

Throughout the centuries since Christ walked this earth, there have been false prophecies—about the time of Christ's return, the nature of His coming, some even claiming He's already come back to earth in secret.

And Jesus predicted this would happen. Listen to what He told His disciples:

> 'Take heed that no one deceives you.' (Matthew 24:4)

This was His FIRST warning when they asked about the end times—even before He warned about wars or famines or earthquakes. The first danger? Deception.

Here's what this means for you: The confusion you feel about prophecy isn't accidental. Jesus predicted there would be many voices, many interpretations, many self-proclaimed experts leading people astray.

Your confusion is actually proof that Jesus' prophecy is coming true. But here's the good news: He warned you about the deception so you could avoid it. You don't have to be swept away by every new theory or sensational prediction.

All those different interpretations of the same event could not be simultaneously correct. This confusion is largely the result of people's private interpretation. We need to let the Bible interpret itself.

Today's confusion may make us anxious—but the answer to our anxiety lies only in "rightly dividing the word of truth" (2 Timothy 2:15). Otherwise, we will heighten the confusion and deepen the darkness.

When Scripture Interprets Scripture, Prophecy Brings Comfort

It's worth repeating: Bible prophecy is a guiding light. It should be understood by letting Scripture interpret its own terms and symbols.

But what does this look like practically?

Here's a simple example: In Revelation 1:20, an angel is explaining John's vision of seven stars and seven lampstands. Does John have to guess what they mean? No. The angel tells him directly: 'The seven stars are the angels of the seven churches, and the seven lampstands are the seven churches.'

The Bible interprets its own symbols. You don't need a prophecy expert to tell you what the stars and lampstands mean—the Bible tells you itself.

Or consider Daniel 7. Daniel sees four beasts rising from the sea—strange, terrifying creatures (verse 3). Does he have to speculate about their meaning? No. Just read the whole thing prayerfully. The angel explains in verse 17: 'Those great beasts, which are four, are four kings which arise out of the earth.'

Again, Scripture interprets itself.

This is how God designed prophecy to work. When you let the Bible define its own terms—when you cross-reference Scripture with Scripture, when you let clear passages illuminate unclear ones—prophecy stops being a mystery and starts being a message.

We must remember that the prophetic writers were "moved by the Holy Spirit" to write. If the Governing influence is the Holy Spirit, then we can expect prophetic clues even across Old and New Testaments.

God is consistent throughout His Word on this principle. For example, reading the book of Daniel illuminates the study in Revelation, and vice versa.

How could a God who wants us to know and understand Him leave us a "puzzle" to make our understanding of Him more confusing? The principle that "Scripture interprets Scripture" helps us avoid errors and false interpretations of Bible prophecies.

Consider the popular teaching about Israel in Bible prophecy. You wouldn't believe how confusing this has become because some Bible students neglect parts of the Bible—using certain scriptures to support someone's "private interpretation."

This is a common source of confusion, so let's take a moment to clarify it biblically.

There is a difference between Israel as a theocracy and Israel created by a UN charter. The nation of Israel to whom God made those promises we read in the Old Testament was broadened to include all peoples—just as God had prophesied to Abraham (Father of many nations).

Do you remember the Biblical account of the Jews (the nation of Israel during and after Christ) rejected the Messiah and even stoned Stephen for believing and preaching Jesus? Well, the gospel then spread to Jews and Gentiles alike—to all peoples.

The Israel of God then became a "spiritual kingdom" of all believers. That's why **Galatians 3:28-29** read like this:

> There is neither Jew nor Greek, there is neither slave nor free, there is neither male nor female; for you are all one in Christ Jesus. [29] And if you are Christ's, then you are Abraham's seed, and heirs according to the promise.

What is this saying? It says, all who belong to Christ have become part of the spiritual "nation" of Israel.

This is crucial for understanding prophecy correctly. When you read Old Testament promises to Israel, you need to ask: Is this about the ethnic nation, or is this about God's spiritual people (the church)? The New Testament gives us the answer.

Many preachers try to fit the spiritual promises and prophecies meant for the people the book of Galatians speaks of to the current nation of Israel. This is not consistent with the terms of the Bible—which says, people of all nations who have accepted Jesus as Messiah have become 'descendants' of Abraham.

And God was not being partial to Abraham, nor was He more in favor of the nation that descended from him over other peoples. Israel was chosen as God's ambassador—they were to represent God to the rest of the world.

Again, listen God's promise to Abraham: "*In your seed **all** the nations of the earth shall be blessed, because you have obeyed My voice.*"

This is a perfect example of the "*Scripture interprets Scripture*" principle. We can understand what transpired in New Testament times by studying what was predicted or said in the Old.

The Galatians 3:28-29 understanding (that spiritual Israel means all believers in Christ) versus the modern political state of Israel is a critical distinction that keeps prophecy interpretation biblically sound rather than sensationalistic. This is exactly the kind of careful scriptural examination that is needed to prevent the fear mongering that is common today.

When we're confident that the same Holy Spirit inspired all of Scripture—from Genesis to Revelation—we can trust that prophecy will bring hope and comfort, not fear and confu-sion.

You've learned WHO prophecy is for (it's for you). You've learned WHAT prophetic peace is (trust in God's proven word). And now you understand WHY prophecy brings peace (because Scripture interprets itself, dispelling confusion).

Now you're ready for the proof. Are you ready to see WHERE God's control shows up in history and current events? Let's turn to the 'H' in our LIGHT framework!

Chapter Four

H - History Proves It: Where We See God's Control in Current Events

Where do we see God's control in current events? How does history prove that prophecy is reliable?

Those are the questions we need to answer. We hear the promises, but we need proof. We want to know: Has God actually done what He said He would do?

The answer is a resounding yes. And the evidence is overwhelming.

Let me show you.

We've seen that Bible prophecy has been **Left for us**—not just for scholars. We've learned that Instead of Panic, we can trust God and enjoy prophetic peace. We've discovered that prophecy was designed to Guide us through the darkness of uncertainty.

Now it's time for the proof. History isn't just a record of what happened—it's a testimony to God's faithfulness. When we look at what God predicted thousands of years ago and compare it to what actually occurred, the evidence becomes undeniable.

Get ready. Now let's see WHERE we may see prophecy unfolding. You will see how it is being fulfilled in current events that are happening around you. You will also recognize that history contains credible proofs that show the prophetic word has unfolded just as God has told us in the Bible.

Daniel 2's Kingdoms—History Proved God's Prophetic Accuracy

Let's start with the big one—the prophecy that skeptics have tried (and failed) to explain away for 2,600 years.

It's found in Daniel chapter 2. Here's the backstory: The Babylonian king, Nebuchadnezzar, had a troubling dream. He couldn't remember it, but he knew it was important. So he demanded his wise men tell him both the dream AND its meaning—or they all die.

Impossible, right? No one can tell someone else what they dreamed.

But Daniel could. Because God revealed it to him.

Daniel described a massive statue the king had seen in his dream: a head of gold, chest and arms of silver, belly and thighs of bronze, legs of iron, and feet of iron mixed with clay. Then a stone—cut without human hands—struck the statue's feet and destroyed it.

Then Daniel did something extraordinary. He told the king what it meant—and named the sequence of world empires that would rule the earth for the next 2,600 years.

History is the witness, and it proves God's prophetic accuracy through His prophets in the Bible. Here's what Daniel predicted, standing in Babylon around 600 BC:

Kingdom 1: **Babylon** (the head of gold) - 'You are this head of gold,' Daniel told Nebuchadnezzar. The current empire.

Kingdom 2: **Medo-Persia** (chest/arms of silver) - 'After you shall arise another kingdom inferior to yours.' Babylon fell to the Medes and Persians in 539 BC, exactly as predicted.

Kingdom 3: **Greece** (belly/thighs of bronze) - 'Then another, a third kingdom of bronze, which shall rule over all the earth.' Alexander the Great conquered Persia in 331 BC.

Kingdom 4: **Rome** (legs of iron) - 'The fourth kingdom shall be as strong as iron.' Rome crushed Greece and ruled the known world.

Divided kingdoms (feet of iron and clay) - 'The kingdom shall be divided... they will not adhere to one another, just as iron does not mix with clay.' Rome fragmented into the **nations of Europe**—which remain divided to this day.

Every single prediction came true. Exactly as Daniel said. In the exact order he named. Over the course of 2,600 years.

In his comment on the accuracy of Bible prophecy, the late preacher Charles D. Brooks made a notable comment. I chose to call his statement, The C.D. Brooks principle. Brooks said, "I love the Bible, and I love the newspaper. I read the Bible to find out what will happen; I read the newspaper to see that it has happened."

That's exactly what we're doing in this chapter. We're opening the newspaper of history and seeing that everything God predicted through Daniel has already happened—exactly as He said it would.

Why did every prediction come true with such precision?

Because Daniel wasn't guessing. He wasn't making educated predictions based on political trends. He was declaring what God had revealed to him:

'The dream is certain, and its interpretation is sure.' (Daniel 2:45)

Certain. Not probable or likely.

Sure. Not speculative.

And 2,600 years of history says AMEN.

Now, I want you to notice something important: It's not like people haven't tried to prove this prophecy wrong. Let's start with the king himself. Nebuchadnezzar didn't like hearing that his kingdom would be replaced. Daniel had just told him, 'You are this head of gold. But after you shall arise another kingdom inferior to yours' (Daniel 2:38-39).

So what did Nebuchadnezzar do? He built his own statue—completely gold from head to toe (Daniel 3:1). No silver. No bronze. No iron. No clay. All gold. All Babylon. Forever.

It was his way of saying, 'I reject your prophecy, Daniel. Babylon will last forever.'

But God's word doesn't change based on human opinion. Babylon fell to Medo-Persia in 539 BC, exactly as Daniel predicted. The king's golden statue couldn't stop it. His defiance couldn't prevent it.

And that's been the pattern ever since.

Failed Attempts to Reunite Rome Prove Daniel 2:43

Now let's fast-forward to modern history. If Daniel 2 is just ancient prediction with no relevance today, we'd expect someone to eventually reunite Europe back into a single empire like Rome, right?

But that hasn't happened. And Daniel told us why 2,600 years ago:

'They will mingle with the seed of men; but they will not adhere to one another, just as iron does not mix with clay.' (Daniel 2:43)

Think about that phrase: 'They will not adhere to one another.' That's not a description of what WAS—it's a prediction of what WOULD BE. A permanent state of division.

And history has proven it true. Over and over and over again.

Let me show you.

Napoleon Bonaparte conquered most of Europe in the early 1800s. He crowned himself emperor and seemed unstoppable. Through military genius and political alliances (including marrying his relatives into European royal families—'they will mingle'), he came closer than anyone since Rome to uniting Europe under one ruler.

He failed. His empire collapsed. Europe remained divided.

Adolf Hitler tried the same thing in the 1940s. His Third Reich conquered nation after nation. He declared it would last a thousand years.

It lasted twelve. Europe remained divided.

The European Union is trying a different approach today—not through military conquest, but through economic and political integration. They share a currency. They've removed borders. They're trying to create a unified Europe through cooperation rather than conquest.

But even they acknowledge it's not working. Brexit. Rising nationalism. Economic tensions between north and south. Political divisions between east and west. They're mingling, but they're not adhering.

According to Daniel 2:43, this will continue. Every human attempt to establish another single global empire like Babylon or Rome will fail. Not because humans aren't trying hard enough, but God said they won't adhere. He sees the end.

These aren't political accidents. They're prophetic fulfillment. You can watch world news today and see God's 'No' in action.

Other Fulfilled Prophecies That Build Our Confidence in God's Word

Here are a few more Bible prophecies that have been fulfilled just as predicted. These accounts help to build faith and confidence in God's prophetic word and give us hope and peace in this chaotic world in which we live today.

Jesus' birthplace: Micah 5:2 predicted Bethlehem as the birthplace of the Messiah some 700 years before it happened. What were the odds for this to happen?

My short answer to this: the odds were extremely low—bordering on impossible—just days before Jesus was born.

First, let's look at the prophecy for context, then I'll explain the odds of that happening were very low.

> "But you, Bethlehem Ephrathah, Though you are little among the thousands of Judah, Yet out of you shall come forth to Me The One to be Ruler in Israel, Whose goings forth are from of old, From everlasting."
>
> Micah 5:2 (NKJV)

Now, see how close to impossible this was?

1. Micah's prophecy was specific in the statement. The verse doesn't just point to the land of Judah. It names Bethlehem Ephrathah, a tiny village. Consider that most messianic expectations in the first century focused on Jerusalem or a powerful military figure. Bethlehem was not the obvious choice.

2. Mary and Joseph didn't live anywhere near Bethlehem. They lived about 90 miles north, in Nazareth—and there were no modes of transportation as we have today! For the prophecy to be fulfilled naturally, a very pregnant woman would have to make a long, difficult journey to a village she had no reason to visit.

3. The journey only happened because of a Roman political event. "How probable?" I hear you saying. The

decree from Caesar Augustus forced them to travel for a census. The timing of that decree wasn't controlled by Israel, Joseph, Mary, or any prophet. It took an empire-wide order to move one couple into the right village.

4. What were the odds—humanly speaking? And this part is speculative, but it still boggles the mind: Historians agree Bethlehem was tiny—likely about 300 to 1,000 residents. Mary and Joseph had no ties there except ancestry. If you describe it like a probability problem:

— Couple lives 90 miles north

— Woman is late-term pregnant

— No natural reason to travel

— Birth window is narrow

— A foreign emperor issues a decree at the exact moment needed

The probability of all that aligning by coincidence is extremely small. It isn't a clean numerical calculation, but it's fair to say it's far less than 1%, probably closer to a tiny fraction of a percent.

If someone tried calculating it as statisticians do with prophecy probabilities (like the classic work by Peter Stoner), Bethlehem's naming alone would be seen as having very low odds of fulfillment without intentional design.

5. Days before the birth of Christ? If you were living in Nazareth the week before:
   — Mary was still in Nazareth
   — No sign they would leave
   — Travel at that stage of pregnancy was unlikely
   — No one knew a decree was coming

Humanly speaking, the odds of getting that couple to Bethlehem just in time were practically zero. But God said it by the prophet Micah, and it happened—just like He said.

Consider some ancient cities whose destruction have remained permanent to this day. History offers a strong reminder that God's words can be trusted. Ancient cities once known for power and wealth—Nineveh, Babylon, and Tyre—fell just as the prophets said they would. Nahum spoke of Nineveh's end, Isaiah warned of Babylon's fall, and Ezekiel foretold Tyre's destruction.

Today, their ruins stand as quiet proof that these prophecies were not guesses. They came to pass with remarkable accuracy. When we see how precisely God's word matched real events, it strengthens our confidence that the Scriptures are reliable. The same God who fulfilled these promises is faithful to every word He gives.

Here's one last one for you—Jerusalem's temple. In Luke 21:6, Jesus warned that the temple in Jerusalem would be completely destroyed, with not one stone left standing. Here are His words to the disciples: "*The days will come in which not one stone shall be left upon another that shall not be thrown down."*—Luke 21:6

Just a generation later, historian Josephus confirmed the devastation was so thorough that visitors could hardly believe a city had ever stood there. This striking fulfillment shows the precision of Jesus' prophetic words. When His prediction matches history so clearly, it strengthens our trust that everything He says carries unshakable truth and authority.

And don't miss the most important prophecies of all—those about the Messiah Himself:

Isaiah 53 predicted a suffering servant who would be 'despised and rejected,' who would be 'wounded for our transgressions,' and who would be 'numbered with the transgressors.' Written 700 years before Christ, this chapter reads like an eyewitness account of Jesus' crucifixion.

Psalm 22 describes crucifixion in graphic detail—'They pierced My hands and My feet... They divide My garments among them, and for My clothing they cast lots'. These prophetic statements were written a thousand years before crucifixion was even invented as a method of execution.

What are the odds of one person fulfilling even eight of the major Messianic prophecies by chance? Mathematician Peter Stoner calculated it at 1 in 10 to the 17th power. That's 1 in 100,000,000,000,000,000.

Jesus fulfilled over 300 Messianic prophecies.

These aren't coincidences. This is the fingerprint of God.

So we've seen God's perfect track record:

- He predicted Bethlehem 700 years early—fulfilled.

- He predicted the destruction of mighty cities—fulfilled.

- He predicted the temple's destruction—fulfilled.

- He predicted the sequence of world empires—fulfilled.

- He predicted Europe would never reunite—being fulfilled right now.

- And the Messianic prophecies? All fulfilled in Jesus Christ.

So here's the question: *Given this track record, shouldn't you trust what God says about the future?*

Current Events Fit the Prophetic Puzzle—The Stone Kingdom Is Next

Given this track record, who would bet against Daniel 2:34, 45? (The stone cut without hands—God's eternal kingdom.) We're narrowing down to today. But let's stand on these two verses from Daniel's prophecy—they carry great significance today. Grasp this and you can watch the news casts with prophetic peace.

So let me ask you: Given God's perfect track record with prophecy—given that He's been 100% accurate for the last 2,600 years—who would bet against the final prediction in Daniel 2?

Here's what Daniel saw:

> "You watched while a stone was cut out without hands, which struck the image on its feet of iron and clay, and broke them in pieces."
>
> —Daniel 2:34 (NKJV)

And here's what it means:

> "In the days of these kings the God of heaven will set up a kingdom which shall never be destroyed; and the kingdom shall not be left to other people; it shall break in pieces and consume all these kingdoms, and it shall stand forever."
>
> —Daniel 2:44 (NKJV)

Think about this: Every metal kingdom came exactly as predicted. Every attempt to reunite them failed exactly as predicted. Every detail has been fulfilled with precision.

So when Daniel says a stone—cut without human hands—will destroy all these kingdoms and establish **God's eternal kingdom**, should you believe it?

Given the evidence, betting against it would be foolish.

Some Bible students suggest Daniel 2 might be pointing to an age of artificial intelligence. Here's their reasoning: First, they see the "iron mixed with clay" as a picture of strength joined with weakness, which they say fits human beings depending on powerful non-human intelligence.

It's necessary to repeat this important principle—*scripture must interpret scripture*. We must read the whole thing. The non-binding amalgamation of iron and clay is explained in verse 43—"*They will mingle with the seed of men; but they will not adhere to one another, just as iron does not mix with clay.*" That's talking about people. All the prophecy from Babylon's reign down through to the divided kingdoms. It's kings and kingdoms.

Second, they argue that this final phase is divided, unstable, and unlike the kingdoms before it—much like today's rapid, disruptive tech shift. Third, they view the rise of machine-driven decision-making as a form of "non-human governance." These ideas are interpretive, and not universal. You should see though that this is quite a stretch.

Verse 44, again... "And in the days of these kings..." Which kings? The kings or kingdoms represented by the toes and feet of iron and clay. How else may we say it? In the reign of these kingdoms that resulted from the breakup of the Roman Empire, the God of heaven will setup a kingdom that will never be destroyed. It will replace all other kingdoms—there's the next universal or global kingdom! Only this is not established by human effort (the stone was cut out or released without hands, i.e. without human help.

So, my fellow end time dweller, all we need to note is the guarantee or surety of this prophecy:

> "Inasmuch as you saw that the stone was cut out of the mountain without hands, and that it broke in pieces the iron, the bronze, the clay, the silver, and the gold-the great God has made known to the king what will come to pass after this. The **dream is certain**, and its **interpretation is sure.**"
>
> —Daniel 2:45 (NKJV)

Today's wars, climate crises, global health emergencies, economic instability—these aren't signs that God lost control. No, He has not. These are signs the final kingdom is approaching. The Stone is about to crush the whole image. The Second Coming of Christ is near.

So here's my question, again: If God fulfilled every prophecy so far with precision, can we trust He'll fulfill the final ones too?

Absolutely.

Not because we're blindly optimistic. Not because we're ignoring reality. But because we've seen the evidence. We've watched God keep every promise. We've seen Him prove Himself faithful for 2,600 years.

The stone is coming, friend. God's eternal kingdom is coming. And just like Babylon, Persia, Greece, Rome, and the divided nations—it will come exactly as He said.

And when that stone strikes—when God's kingdom is established—the Morning Star will rise. Not just in the sky, but in the hearts of all who have trusted Him. Jesus declared in Revelation 22:16: '*I am the Root and the Offspring of David, the Bright and Morning Star.*'

This is what Peter meant when he said prophecy is 'a light that shines in a dark place, until the day dawns and the morning star rises in your hearts' (2 Peter 1:19). The light of prophecy guides us through the darkness of uncertainty. But it's not just pointing to itself—it's pointing to HIM. To the One who is coming. To the dawn that will end all darkness.

That's not wishful thinking. That's prophetic certainty.

And that's why you can watch today's news headlines with peace instead of panic.

Chapter Five

T - Trust God's Timeline: When Events Unfold and How to Watch Without Panicking

WHEN will these prophetic events happen? And HOW can you watch current events unfold without panicking?

Those are probably the two questions believers in the end time ask most often. We want to know WHEN Jesus is coming back. We want to know HOW to live in the tension between 'soon' and 'I don't know the day or hour.'

This final chapter of our LIGHT framework addresses both questions—because they're really two sides of the same coin.

Some days the news headlines feel like they're shouting at us. A global pandemic that shut down the world. A war in Europe threatening to spill wider—and similar strife in Africa and elsewhere. Record heatwaves and disasters that make the planet feel fragile. And headlines like this: 'Doomsday Clock moves closer to midnight amid threats of climate change, nuclear war, pandemics, AI.'

It's no wonder many believers read the news and quietly question, "Is this it? Are we close to the end?"

We Want to Know "When"—But Jesus Gave Us Something Better

Let's be honest: We desperately want to know WHEN.

The disciples felt the same way. After Jesus told them the temple would be destroyed, they asked the exact question we tend to ask today: *'Tell us, when will these things be? And what will be the sign of Your coming and of the end of the age?'* (Matthew 24:3)

Notice what they're asking: WHEN and WHAT SIGN. They want specifics. They want a timeline. They want to know the date.

And Jesus didn't give them one.

Instead, He gave them something far more valuable: He gave them SIGNS to watch for (wars, earthquakes, false prophets, the gospel preached to all nations). He gave them WARN-

INGS about deception. He gave them ENCOURAGEMENT to endure. He gave them PERSPECTIVE that these things 'must come to pass' before the end.

But the very first thing—before signs, before warnings, before anything else—He said this:

> **'Take heed that no one deceives you.'**
> —Matthew 24:4

Think about that. When the disciples asked 'WHEN?', Jesus' first response wasn't about timing—it was about deception.

Now, you might think Jesus was evading their question. Why not just tell them the date?

But Jesus wasn't being evasive—He was being protective. He knew that between His ascension and His return, the greatest danger wouldn't be missing the date. It would be being deceived by false christs who claim to have returned.

> "For many will come in My name, saying, 'I am Christ,' and will **deceive** many."
> —Matthew 24:5

And that's exactly what's happened. Throughout church history, false teachers have come saying they're Christ. For example, Allan John Miller (AJ) claims to be Jesus Christ. And

Harold Camping convinced thousands that Jesus would return on May 21, 2011. He was wrong.

Many preachers have declared, *'We are the final generation!'* Only to die, and the world continues.

And every failed prediction does two things: First, it makes **unbelievers mock** the faith. Second, it makes some **believers anxious** and confused.

This is why the confusion and fear exist today. Not because prophecy is unclear, but because we've ignored Jesus' warning. We've listened to too many self-proclaimed 'prophets.' We've followed too many conflicting interpretations. We've been deceived by too much speculation masquerading as biblical truth.

It may seem like Jesus was evading their question, but the Savior is never rude. Instead, He was trying to protect them from being destroyed by wolves—false prophets and teachers.

The confusion and fear associated with prophecy today exists because we've ignored this warning—too many "prophets," too many conflicting interpretations, too much deception. Many people don't know what to believe anymore. And many unsuspecting followers have been led to believe, what Peter calls, "cunningly devised fables."

So if you wonder about the many different voices, teachings, and interpretations on current events—if the news headlines make your brain "spin" and wonder if we're seeing the end of the world, don't panic.

God isn't pacing the floor. He isn't surprised, shaken, or late. The same Lord who guided His people through every generation invites you to watch the times—prayerfully read His word, and find His prophetic peace.

So if Jesus didn't give us exact dates, and if trying to figure them out has led to confusion and deception, what DID He give us? How ARE we supposed to live in the meantime?

"The Just Shall Live by Faith"—Not by Full Knowledge

The prophet Habakkuk taught it (Old Testament), Paul the Apostle repeated it (New Testament)—faith is how we're designed to relate to God. (see Habakkuk 2:4, Romans 1:17, Galatians 3:11, and Hebrews 10:38. All these references give the same reminder.)

But here's something very noteworthy—in Hebrews 10, the statement (the just shall live by faith, or by his faith) is linked to the promise and prophecy of Christ's Second Coming. Even though we don't know exactly when, faithful believers still sense the imminence and the urgency of the promise in the prophecy.

"For yet a little while, And He who is coming will come and will not tarry. [38] Now **the just shall live**

by faith; But if anyone draws back, My soul has no pleasure in him."

— Hebrews 10:37-38 NKJV

Did you catch that? In other words, we've got to have faith in the promise—full knowledge and understanding of what's happening around us is unnecessary.

But why would God design it this way? Why not just tell us everything?

Because if we knew all the details of our future—every trial, every tragedy, every triumph—we wouldn't need faith. We'd engineer our own destinies. We'd try to avoid the hard parts and rush to the good parts. We'd manipulate circumstances rather than trust God through them.

And in doing that, we'd lose **the very thing God values most: our relationship with Him.**

Faith isn't just believing God exists. It's trusting Him when you can't see the path ahead. It's clinging to His promises when circumstances scream the opposite. It's the foundation of relationship—and **God wants a faith relationship with you more than He wants you to have information**.

God Has Not Changed, And His Promises Remain Sure

Think about what we've learned in this book:

- God predicted Babylon would fall to Persia—it did.

- God predicted Jesus would be born in Bethlehem—He was.

- God predicted Rome would fragment and never reunite—it hasn't.

- God predicted Jerusalem's temple would be destroyed—it was.

Every single promise kept. Every single prophecy fulfilled. Over thousands of years.

The God who spoke Jeremiah 29:11 ('I know the plans I have for you') is the same 'Our Father' we pray to today. He's alive, and He hasn't reneged on a single promise.

And here's what this means for today's headlines: *Current events may seem chaotic, but they align perfectly with God's end-time timeline.* There's no need to fear because God is still in control—just as He's been in control for the past 2,600 years of fulfilled prophecy.

Our heavenly Father is always faithful. Look at one of the ways the writer of Hebrews states this:

> Let us hold fast the confession of our hope without wavering, for **He who promised is faithful**.
>
> — Hebrews 10:23 (NKJV)

Again, there's no need to fear because God is in control. But how do we get the faith to latch on to that?

We get faith by daily reading His Word (Romans 10:17)—this is HOW a fearful, sometimes-conflicted, ordinary individual like you and me builds confidence: consistent time in Scripture.

> So then faith comes by hearing, and hearing by the word of God.
> — Romans 10:17 (NKJV)

This is HOW you build confidence. Not through watching more news. Not through following more prophecy teachers. Not through obsessing over current events.

Through consistent time in Scripture.

Here's what this looks like practically: Start each morning reading one chapter from the Gospels or the Psalms. Before you check the news, check in with God. Before you scroll through headlines that stir anxiety, saturate your mind with His promises that bring peace.

Ten minutes a day. That's all it takes to start shifting from panic to peace.

How to Live "*Almost There*" Without Anxiety—Practical Daily Tools

We're like kids on a road trip asking, "Are we there yet?"—it's natural, we're human, but there's a better way. So, here's a little bit of advice from a fellow traveler who really believes that the Bible prophecies are sure, God hasn't abandoned us, and the horrific news headlines are reminders that God's promises are true.

1. Check every news event and prophetic interpretation against Scripture (be wary of sensational predictions); let the Bible interpret itself; if God hasn't revealed it, don't theorize it.

2. Our major concern shouldn't be, "Are we there yet?" but "Do I know Him better today than yesterday?"—shift from timeline obsession to relationship pursuit.

Biblical Assurances to Calm Your Specific Fears

Can we trust God's timeline through the headlines? Can we watch these end times events unfold across our TV screens and play out on social media without panicking?

Dear reader, we can.

You must realize that God has NOT lost control of His universe and that He does things in His timing—something we humans living in a push-button age fail to grasp sometimes.

Let me address five specific fears I hear from believers—with biblical answers that bring peace.

Assurance #1: The World Will NOT End in Nuclear Holocaust

When you see news about nuclear threats, rising global tensions, or doomsday scenarios, remember this:

The Bible says people will be alive when Jesus returns.

> 'For the Lord Himself will descend from heaven with a shout... and the dead in Christ will rise first. Then we who are alive and remain shall be caught up together with them in the clouds...'
>
> 1 Thessalonians 4:16-17

An in the last book of the Bible, we read this reminder:

> 'Behold, He is coming with clouds, and every eye will see Him.'
>
> Revelation 1:7

Think about those phrases:

'*We who are alive and remain*'—there will be living people.

'*Every eye will see Him*'—there will be people to see.

If total nuclear annihilation wiped out humanity before Jesus' return, these prophecies would be false. And we've already established in Chapter 4 that God's prophecies don't fail.

So when you hear nuclear threats, remember: God's Word guarantees there will be people here when Jesus comes. The world won't end with a mushroom cloud. It will end with the King of Kings descending in glory.

This isn't wishful thinking—it's prophetic certainty.

Assurance #2: God's Final Kingdom Is as Real as Babylon, Persia, Greece, and Rome

Every kingdom named in the prophecy of Daniel 2 was literal, physical, and historical—why would the final one be different?

According to Daniel 2:34, 44, and 45, the stone kingdom will be just as real as the empires that came before. The difference? It will not be established by human effort, nor will be governed by humans.

Hey! This will be God's eternal kingdom.

> And in the days of these kings **the God of heaven will set up a kingdom** which **shall never be destroyed**; and the kingdom **shall not be left to other people**; it shall break in pieces and con-

sume all these kingdoms, and it **shall stand forever**.

> —Daniel 2:44 (NKJV)

Don't let anyone spiritualize away God's promise of a literal, eternal kingdom on earth. Hold on to your prophetic peace.

Assurance #3: Not Every "Mark of the Beast" Interpretation Can Be True—Jesus Warned About This

The many conflicting interpretations on the Mark of the Beast prove Jesus' warning about false prophets was accurate (Matthew 24:11, 24).

Again, God can explain Himself—we must let scripture interpret itself. Read the whole thing. Let Scripture define "the mark," as well as "the beast". We cannot just swallow the interpretations of sensational preachers or YouTube videos that may be positing "cunningly devised fables."

If interpretations contradict each other, can they all be correct? Most (or all) those conflicting positions are wrong. We've got to stick with what the Bible clearly says.

So what CAN we know about the mark of the beast from Scripture alone?

Without getting into all the details (that's a whole other book!), here's what Revelation 13-14 makes clear:

- It's connected to **worship** of the beast (Revelation 13:15-16)

- It's a deliberate choice, not an accident (Revelation 14:9 warns against receiving it)

- It's placed on the forehead or hand (Revelation 13:16)

- Those who refuse it face persecution (Revelation 13:17)

- Those who obey God's commandments and resist the mark are blessed (Revelation 14:12)

What does this tell us? The mark is ultimately about allegiance and worship. It's about who you serve—God or the beast. It's about faithfulness and patient endurance under pressure.

So instead of obsessing over technology, microchips, or barcodes, focus on this: Are you faithful to God today? Do you worship Him alone? Are you willing to stand for truth even when it's unpopular or costly?

If the answer is yes, you don't need to fear the mark. Your allegiance is already settled.

Assurance #4: See That You Are Not Troubled

Listen to Jesus' words in Matthew 24 again:

'And you will hear of wars and rumors of wars. See that you are not troubled; for all these things must come to pass, but the end is not yet.' (Matthew 24:6)

Jesus said, "*See that you are not troubled*" (Matthew 24:6). That was His advice for believers who would experience wars, rumors of wars, pandemics, economic collapse—Jesus predicted all of it AND commanded us not to be troubled. Those events are signs that Christ warned us about.

God's presence with you is more certain than tomorrow's headlines (Hebrews 13:5, Matthew 28:20). The promise to never leave you nor forsake you is sure—He said, "**I am with you always, even to the end of the age.**" That's blessed assurance.

Your peace doesn't depend on political stability; it depends on God's unchanging promise.

Peter calls the prophetic promises, "**a more sure word of prophecy,**" (2 Peter 1:19 KJV.) It is light in a dark place.

Assurance #5: Date-Setters and False Christs Prove Jesus' Prophecy, Not Their Own

Jesus repeatedly predicted false christs and false prophets would come, (Matthew 24:5, 11, and 24).

> For false christs and false prophets will rise and show great signs and wonders to deceive, if possible, even the elect.
>
> Matthew 24:24 NKJV

Even with this unmistakable warning, there are people in the world at this moment, claiming they are Christ. Worst—several others believe them.

He also said even angels don't know the day or hour (Mark 13:32)—so anyone claiming to know when Christ will come (or that He has already come) is already proven wrong.

Every failed date prediction should increase your confidence in Jesus' words, not shake it, because Christ has prophesied it.

These assurances aren't just about surviving until Jesus returns. They're about living with confident expectation of the day when 'the morning star rises' (2 Peter 1:19)—when Christ establishes His kingdom and darkness ends forever.

Here are four practical tools:

Tool #1: Check Events Against Scripture, Not Sensational Predictions

When you hear a prophecy teacher make a dramatic claim, don't ask 'Does this sound exciting?' Ask: 'What does the BIBLE say about this?'

Open your Bible. Read the passage they're referencing. Pray for the Holy Spirit who inspired the Bible writers to help you see truth. See if their interpretation matches what Scripture actually says. If it doesn't, reject the teaching—no matter how popular the teacher.

Tool #2: Let the Bible Interpret Itself

We've said this throughout the book, but here's how to apply it daily:

- When you encounter a confusing prophetic passage, look for other places Scripture addresses the same topic.

- Use a concordance or Bible app to find related verses

- Compare clear passages with unclear ones

- Trust what the Bible explains plainly over human speculation

Tool #3: Don't Theorize What God Hasn't Revealed

If Scripture is silent or unclear on a detail, it's okay to say 'I don't know.' You don't have to have an opinion on every prophetic detail. Resist the urge to fill in gaps with speculation.

Remember: **Faith isn't knowing everything. It's trusting the One who does**.

Tool #4: Focus on Knowing HIM, Not Just Knowing the Timeline

Here's the most important tool: **Make relationship with your Savior your priority**.

Instead of asking 'When is Jesus coming?' ask 'Am I growing closer to Him today?' Instead of obsessing over signs, focus on becoming more like Him. Instead of fearing the future, trust the One who holds it.

Because here's the truth: When you truly know Him—when you've experienced His faithfulness, His love, His presence—the timeline matters less. You're not anxious about WHEN He's coming because you're confident in WHO is coming.

You've completed the journey through the LIGHT framework.

You've learned that prophecy was **Left for Us**—it's your birthright as a believer, not reserved for scholars.

You've discovered that **Instead of Panic**, you can have prophetic peace by trusting God's sure word.

You've understood that prophecy **Guides us through the darkness**, dispelling confusion when we let Scripture interpret itself.

You've seen that **History Proves It**—God has kept every prophetic promise He has made, and in particular, those for the last 2,600 years on which we have focused. So you can trust the years still ahead.

And now you have the tools to **Trust God's timeline**, watching current events unfold with confidence instead of fear.

You're no longer the anxious person sitting on the couch, paralyzed by terrifying headlines.

You're equipped. You're informed. You're anchored in God's unchanging Word.

You have prophetic peace.

And in the next chapter, I want to send you out with one final encouragement; that is, a call to live boldly in light of what you now know.

CONCLUSION: The LIGHT Is On—Walk in Prophetic Peace

R emember when you started this book?

You were sitting on your couch (possibly), your favorite drink growing cold, watching the evening news. Another war. Another economic crisis. Another "expert" on YouTube explaining how this latest event proved we're living in the end times. Your stomach was tight. Your mind was racing.

You reached for your Bible—maybe Revelation, maybe Daniel—hoping for answers. But the symbols confused you. The beasts and numbers and seals felt like a code you didn't have the key to unlock. And you weren't just anxious about the news anymore; you were anxious about not understanding the very book that was supposed to bring you comfort.

That might have been you at the beginning of this book. Do you remember that feeling?

But Something Has Changed

Something profound has shifted. You have changed.

You're not the same person who opened this book with "trembling" hands and a troubled heart. Look at what you know now that you didn't know before:

You discovered that prophecy is FOR you—not reserved for scholars with advanced degrees or prophecy "experts" with complicated charts. It's **a gift from your Father** who loves you too much to leave you in the dark about His plans.

You learned that the chaos **proves God's control**, not His absence. Every war, every crisis, every headline that once made you panic is actually evidence (a sign) that God's prophetic Word is unfolding exactly as He said it would.

You understand that **Scripture interprets itself**. You don't need a self-proclaimed guru or the latest bestselling prophecy book to decode God's Word. When you let the Bible define its own terms and cross-reference its own symbols, clarity replaces confusion. Light dispels darkness.

You've seen undeniable historical proof. Daniel predicted the succession of world empires 2,600 years ago—Babylon, Medo-Persia, Greece, Rome, and the divided nations of Europe. Every single prediction came true with perfect precision. God's track record is flawless, which means **you can trust the promises** still ahead.

You have practical tools. You're no longer helpless when you turn on the news. You know how to check events against Scripture, let the Bible interpret itself, avoid speculation, and focus on knowing God rather than obsessing over timelines.

You're not the same person who opened this book.

You've been transformed from an anxious news-watcher into a confident truth-holder. From prophetic panic to prophetic peace.

The LIGHT Framework: Your Foundation

Let's walk through what you've learned one final time—not to repeat ourselves, but to anchor these truths deep in your heart.

L - Left for Us

You discovered that prophecy isn't a mystery for the elite—it's a gift from your Father who loves you. Revelation 1:3 promises a blessing to those who read and heed the prophecy of that book. It was left specifically for you, God's beloved child, so you could know His plans and find peace in His promises.

I - Instead of Panic

You learned that prophetic peace comes from trusting God's proven Word. Every fulfilled prophecy—from Bethlehem to

Babylon's fall to Rome's fragmentation—is a deposit guaranteeing He'll keep the promises still ahead.

The research confirms what Scripture teaches: uncertainty intensifies fear, but **God gave prophecy to calm our fears** by unpacking the unknown with grace and love.

G - Guiding Through Darkness

You understood that confusion comes from ignoring God's method—letting Scripture interpret itself. When people use "private interpretation" (2 Peter 1:20), they create the very darkness and fear God intended prophecy to dispel. But when you **let the Bible explain its own symbols** and cross-reference its own passages, prophecy becomes what God designed it to be: **a guiding light through dark times**.

H - History Proves It

You saw overwhelming evidence that God has kept every prophetic promise with perfect precision. **Kingdoms rose and fell exactly as Daniel predicted**. Cities were destroyed exactly as Isaiah and Ezekiel foretold. Jesus was born in Bethlehem exactly as Micah declared 700 years earlier. Jerusalem's temple was demolished exactly as Jesus warned. Napoleon failed. Hitler failed. The EU cannot reunite Europe. **God's track record is perfect**—which means His future promises are certain.

T - Trusting Through the Headlines

You received practical tools to watch current events through the lens of Scripture. You learned that Jesus didn't give His disciples exact dates because He gave them something better—warnings about deception, signs to watch for, and the command "See that you are not troubled" (Matthew 24:6). You understand now that faith, not full knowledge, is how God designed us to relate to Him. And you have five specific biblical assurances that address your deepest fears about the future.

These five principles—this LIGHT framework—are now yours to keep.

They're not just information you learned. They're a lens through which you now see the world. They're a foundation on which you can stand firm when everything else shakes.

What Now? Your Three Actions

So what do you do with what you've learned? How do you live differently because of this book?

Here are **three** clear actions:

Action #1: Share the Light

You know something millions of anxious believers desperately need to know.

All around you are people sitting on their couches, watching the same headlines you watch, feeling the same anxiety you used to feel. They're listening to conflicting "experts" and drowning in prophetic panic.

You have a gift to give them.

When someone says they're anxious about end times, you can say, "Let me show you something that brought me peace." Share the LIGHT framework. Recommend this book. Teach them that prophecy is for them, that the chaos proves God's in control, that Scripture interprets itself, that history proves God's faithfulness, and that they can trust His time-line.

You don't need to be pushy or preachy. Just share your story. Tell them how you moved from fear to faith. Invite them into the peace you've found.

The world is full of people stumbling in prophetic darkness. You know where the light switch is. Show them.

Action #2: Keep Growing in the Word

This book is a beginning, not an ending.

You've learned the framework, but there's so much more to discover. Continue your daily time in Scripture. Remember Romans 10:17: "*Faith comes by hearing, and hearing by the word of God.*" Every day you spend in God's Word, your faith grows stronger, and your peace grows steadier.

Now that you understand the principles, go deeper into the prophetic books. Study Daniel with fresh eyes. Read Revelation with confidence instead of confusion. Explore Isaiah, Ezekiel, Zechariah. Let Scripture interpret Scripture. Cross-reference passages. Watch how the Old Testament illuminates the New and vice versa.

Every time you read prophecy now, you'll see God's faithfulness, not fear. You'll see His promises, not panic. You'll see light, not darkness.

Make this a lifestyle, not just a one-time learning experience. Let prophetic peace become your new normal.

Action #3: Live as a Witness

Your peace in chaotic times will make people ask questions.

When the next crisis hits—and it will—and everyone around you is spiraling into fear, your calm confidence will stand out. When coworkers are doomscrolling through apocalyptic headlines, and you're at peace, they'll notice. When family members are panicking about wars and rumors of wars, and you're quoting Matthew 24:6 with a smile, they'll wonder what you know that they don't.

> "And you will hear of wars and rumors of wars. See that you are not troubled; for all these things must come to pass, but the end is not yet."
> —Jesus, in Matthew 24:6

You're not just learning about prophetic peace—you're becoming a living testimony of it. Peter knew this journey as a witness better than anyone.

He witnessed the Transfiguration, saw Moses and Elijah, and heard God's voice thundered from heaven: "This is My beloved Son." In that moment, Peter wanted to stay there forever—to build shelters and never leave. It was so beautiful, so eternally peaceful...

But Jesus brought him and his fellow disciples back down the mountain. Why?

Because Peter's calling wasn't to stay in the "preview"—it was to share the **hope** of that glory with others. He was to tell believers like you and me scattered across the world: "I saw it. The Morning Star is real. The dawn is coming." And that's what he did in 2 Peter 1:16-19. He gave his eyewitness testimony of the glory of the Coming of the Lord.

And now, that's your calling too.

First Peter 3:15 says, "*Always be ready to give a defense to everyone who asks you a reason for the hope that is in you.*" People will ask. Your unexplainable peace in troubling times will provoke questions. Be ready with an answer.

Not a complicated theological lecture. Not a chart with timelines and beasts. Just this: "I've learned to see current events through the lens of God's prophetic Word. He's in control. He's keeping His promises. And that gives me peace."

That's the witness the world needs right now.

The Promise: God Is With You

As you walk forward in prophetic peace, remember these promises:

Jesus said, "*I am with you always, even to the end of the age*" (Matthew 28:20). He didn't promise the journey would be easy or the headlines would get better. But He promised His presence. Always. Even—especially—in the chaos of the last days.

The writer of Hebrews declared, "*I will never leave you nor forsake you*" (Hebrews 13:5). When the world feels like it's falling apart, God is not pacing the floor of heaven, wringing His hands, wondering what to do. He's right there with you. Steady. Faithful. Unchanging.

Paul reminded us, "*The peace of God, which surpasses all understanding, will guard your hearts and minds through Christ Jesus*" (Philippians 4:6-7). This isn't a peace that depends on circumstances. It's a supernatural peace that makes no logical sense to the world—a peace that surpasses understanding. And it's yours.

The same God who revealed prophetic timelines to Daniel is the same God walking with you today. The same God who kept every promise for 2,600 years is the same God holding your tomorrow. The same God who spoke the world into existence is the same God who speaks peace to your anxious heart.

He who began a good work in you will complete it (Philippians 1:6). This journey of moving from fear to faith isn't over—it's just beginning.

The Vision: Your New Normal

Imagine this:

Tomorrow morning, you turn on the news. Another crisis. Another headline screaming chaos. Wars escalating. Economies tumbling. Politicians deadlocked. Disasters multiplying.

But this time, something is different.

Instead of your stomach tightening, you remember: God predicted this. He's not surprised. He's still in control. This is all part of the plan He outlined thousands of years ago.

Instead of reaching for your phone to doomscroll through more anxiety-inducing headlines, you reach for your Bible. You open to a prophetic passage—maybe Daniel 2, maybe Revelation 19, maybe Matthew 24—and instead of confusion, you see clarity. You see God's faithfulness. You see His promises unfolding exactly as He said.

Instead of anxiety stealing your peace, you feel it—that supernatural calm of Philippians 4:7. A peace that doesn't make sense given the circumstances. A peace that surpasses all understanding.

You sip from your cup again. You take a deep breath. And you whisper with confidence: "Right on schedule. God's still in control."

This is your new normal.

Not because the world got safer. Not because the news got better. Not because the crises stopped coming.

But because YOU changed.

You learned to see current events through the lens of God's prophetic Word. You learned to let Scripture interpret itself instead of being tossed around by every new "expert" inter-pretation. You learned that history proves God's faithfulness and that His track record guarantees His future promises.

You're living in the light now.

And when people around you ask—and they will ask—how you can have such peace when the world is falling apart, you'll have an answer.

You'll tell them about the LIGHT framework. You'll tell them about a God who keeps His promises. You'll tell them about prophetic peace.

And maybe—just maybe—you'll help them find the light switch too.

Turn On the Light—Until the Dawn Breaks

Peter said the prophetic word is "a light that shines in a dark place" (2 Peter 1:19).

You've learned how to turn on that light. But remember: **the light isn't the destination—it's the guide.** It's pointing you toward something greater. Someone greater.

Jesus Christ, the Bright and Morning Star (Revelation 22:16), is coming. When He returns to establish His eternal kingdom, every heart that has loved Him and walked by faith will experience the fulfillment of every prophetic promise. The dawn will break. The darkness will end. And the Morning Star will rise—not just in the sky, but in the hearts of all His faithful people.

That's what you're living for. That's what prophecy is pointing toward. That's why you have peace even in the darkest times.

The light is on. But the dawn is coming.

Walk in prophetic peace—until the day dawns.

The switch was always there. God installed it thousands of years ago through His prophets—Daniel, Isaiah, Ezekiel, Zechariah, and ultimately through His Son, Jesus Christ. The light has been shining all along, illuminating the path from darkness to dawn, from chaos to the coming kingdom.

You just didn't know where to find the switch.

Now you do.

You know that prophecy was left for you. You know that it brings peace, not panic. You know that it guides through darkness by interpreting itself. You know that history proves its reliability. And you know how to trust God's timeline while watching current events unfold.

The light is on.

Now, keep it shining. Not just for yourself, but for everyone around you still stumbling in the dark. Be the person who doesn't panic when the headlines scream. Be the voice of calm when others are spiraling. Be the testimony of God's faithfulness when the world questions His presence.

Walk in it. Let prophetic peace define how you live, how you think, how you respond to crisis.

Live in it. Make this your new normal—not occasional peace when circumstances align, but constant peace because God's promises never fail.

Share it. Light isn't meant to be hidden. When you find a light switch in a dark room, you don't keep it to yourself. You turn it on so everyone can see.

The world is darker than ever. Headlines are more terrifying. Crises are multiplying. Anxiety is epidemic.

But you have the light.

You know where the switch is. You know how to turn it on. You know how to walk by its illumination even when everything around you is pitch black.

That's prophetic peace.

And it's not just for you. It's for everyone who's willing to stop stumbling in the dark and start walking in the light.

So go.

Watch the news without panicking.

Read prophecy without confusion.

Live with confidence in God's sovereign plan. It's now your turn to say: "**Don't be afraid. I know where the light is. Let me show you.**"

The LIGHT is on.

Walk — in prophetic peace.